Zion National Park

Zion is a blend of nature's extremes from eroded sandstone to open meadows and sheer walled canyons. Here is a Park where you can be in the middle of it all and see the power of erosion in all directions.

Zion — *the rising walls of stone remind us that we are witness at a point in time, of an age old process — that started in the millennia and obviously will continue for eons to come.*

Zion National Park, located in southern Utah, was first set aside in 1909 as Mukuntuweap National Monument, to preserve dramatic canyons and cliffs caused by erosive forces.

Front cover: Angels Landing, photo by Jeff Gnass. Inside front cover: Autumn's magnificence, photo by David Muench. Page 1: Mt. Carmel Route, photo by Pat O'Hara. Pages 2/3: Towers of the Virgin, photo by Gail Bandini. Pages 4/5: Canyon overlook on east rim, photo by Peter L. Kresan. Pages 6/7: Court of the Patriarchs, photo by Russ Finley.

Edited by Cheri C. Madison.
Book design by K. C. DenDooven.

Seventh Printing, 2009 • New Version

in pictures ZION Nature's Continuing Story®
© 1989 KC PUBLICATIONS, INC.

"in pictures ... Nature's Continuing Story®";
the Eagle / Flag icon on Front Cover are registered
in the U.S. Patent and Trademark Office.

LC 89-45017. ISBN 978-0-88714-031-0.

in pictures

Zion
Nature's Continuing Story®

by Victor L. Jackson

Vic Jackson, a graduate of Wheaton College, Illinois, served as Chief Park Naturalist at Zion National Park from 1973 until his retirement in 1988. Vic, in 1982, was the first recipient of the prestigous NPCA-Freeman Tilden Outstanding Interpreter of the Year Award.

...the Story of Zion National Park

JEFF GNASS

The towering cliffs and deep canyons of Zion National Park give dramatic testament to the twin forces of uplift and erosion. Located along the southwestern edge of the Colorado Plateau, Zion presents some of the most colorfully spectacular scenery anywhere on earth. Shortly after it was first described and photographed in the mid-19th century, artists, photographers, and writers made the arduous journey to see for themselves this chromatic spectacle of the western American landscape. Today it is one of the most visited national parks in the world, its fame only growing in stature as new visitors continue to be awed by the majesty of this geologic wonderland.

With over 5,000 feet of vertical relief, Zion has a remarkable amount of plant and animal diversity within its boundaries. An excellent system of roads and trails makes it easy for the visitor to explore the large diversity of life zones found here.

On the very top are forested plateaus offering wide-ranging vistas of distant mountains and canyons and the opportunity to view elk, deer, and—rarely—cougar. Deep down

Zion Canyon is a place of wonderment and exploration for all. From vehicle turn-out viewpoints; to flat paved trails; to more adventurous hikes; and on, into The Narrows that requires fording the Virgin River — there are places to visit and ways for all to see the many aspects of this magnificent Park — Zion.

"... new VISITORS continue to be *awed* by the majesty of THIS Geologic Wonderland."

in the canyon bottoms, where direct sunlight shines only rarely, there are natural springs and seeps, which provide a habitat for ferns, grasses, flowers, and a variety of trees. The lowest sections of the Park are occupied by dry desert badlands where salt-resistant shrubs and cactus share the blistered landscape with roadrunners, snakes, lizards, and coyotes. Except for the very highest sections of the Park, Zion has a mild climate year-round that invites the exploration of its many wonders.

K.C. DenDooven
Publisher

PAT O'HARA

The East Rim Trail starts at Weeping Rock and quickly climbs above it into a drier west-facing habitat suitable for junipers and a variety of hardy shrubs. Plant species respond dramatically to even slight differences in moisture and slope orientation.

LYNN CHAMBERLAIN

The ringtail cat is common in the cliff areas of the park at the lower elevations. This small mammal is similar to the raccoon, to which it is closely related. The name "cat" was given by miners and others who noted the ringtails' nocturnal habits and their ability to catch mice and other small animals

Zion

Zion is on the western edge of the Colorado Plateau, which stretches from the Great Basin Desert of Nevada to the western slope of the Rocky Mountains. About 25 million years ago, the plateau began to rise thousands of feet out of the sea in a series of stages. Higher terrain attracted more rain and snowfall. This added volume to streams and rivers which now flowed faster down the steeper slopes. The relatively soft sedimentary rocks wore down rapidly along geologic fractures creating the many canyons we now see.

The Virgin River is the main erosional force sculpturing the Zion Canyon we admire. Much of the work may have been done during the Ice Age of a million years ago when precipitation was greater. Spring run-off and summer thundershowers continue to carve an ever changing canyon of spectacular shapes.

The Watchman stands guard at the entrance of Zion Canyon, rising over 2,500 feet above the Virgin River. This river starts on the Markagunt Plateau at 9,000 feet and flows southwest through the park 145 miles to Lake Mead at an elevation of less than 1,000 feet.

The Virgin River Narrows has aroused the interest and imagination of many. This gorge cut through the Navajo Sandstone starts at the Temple of Sinawava and extends about 12 miles upstream. Those wading the river are awed by the soaring rock walls that tower 2,000 feet in the deepest part and come together as close as 18 feet. Be sure to acquire full information at a visitor center about a trip into the Narrows due to changing weather and water conditions. Late June through late September is generally the best time of year for this hike.

JEFF GNASS

*P*ark scenery is never fixed in stone. In April 1995, approximately 250,000 cubic yards of rock and soil tumbled 500 feet down the east wall of Zion Canyon, destroying a section of road leading to Zion Lodge. The forces of canyon formation continue their work, offering spectacular scenic views for generations to come.

GARY LADD

*T*hose hiking along the Angels Landing Trail are rewarded with views of Perpendicular cliffs of Navajo Sandstone colored red from iron oxide located within the rock or precipitated from sources above. As you climb into the relative cool of Refrigerator Canyon, you will find ponderosa pines which normally grow only at higher elevations. A series of sharp switchbacks called Walters Wiggles lifts you to the brink of Scout Lookout.

*T*he hike to Observation Point starts at Weeping Rock just below the contact between the Kayenta and Navajo Sandstone formations and climbs over 2,100 feet to a viewpoint that vividly illustrates the erosional work carried on by the Virgin River. As the softer Kayenta rocks are eroded, they form steep slopes that ultimately undermine the nearly vertical sandstone cliffs. Portions of the cliffs collapse along pre-existing fractures as they lose support, and thus the cliffs are perpetuated as the canyon widens downstream.

JOSEF MUENCH

The Great White Throne, one of the most popular landmarks in the park, rises over 2,400 feet above Zion Canyon. Most of its mass is made up of Navajo Sandstone. The top has less iron oxide, so it is whiter than the base. This formation assumes new beauty when seen through the veil of water dripping from Weeping Rock.

In the lesser known middle part of Zion flows the Left Fork of North Creek, carving an idyllic canyon along ancient geologic joints or fractures in the rock. Soon after emerging from The Subway, a remarkable rock reminder of far off cities, it descends many broken layers of rock known as Archangel Cascades. Only off-trail routes lead to these features.

LARRY ULRICH

Afternoon thundershowers are common from mid-July through August. In the slickrock areas of the park, such as along both sides of Clear Creek, rainwater is only slightly absorbed, with most of it running rapidly off the Navajo Sandstone into the nearest drainage. The moisture that does remain from rain and snow storms supports vegetation in niches on the rock and along the stream courses. Ponderosa pines are found in the higher portions of the park, with cottonwoods common along drainages.

Checkerboard Mesa is a prominent feature as you enter the park from the east. The near horizontal lines originated as bedding planes while the sand grains were blown about in giant dunes millions of years ago. After the land submerged beneath the sea, calcium carbonate percolated through the sand dunes, later cementing them together as sandstone. As the land slowly rose and thousands of feet of rock were eroded away, vertical fractures developed, which have been enlarged by run-off from rains and melting snows.

Near Checkerboard Mesa is a virtual fantasyland of strange shapes. Distinctive characteristics of this vast exposure of Navajo Sandstone are the bedding planes etched by wind and water. Cross bedding occurs where ancient winds changed direction and thus layered sand at a variety of angles, often intersecting with each other. After being transformed into sandstone by pressures and cementing agents deep in the earth, the land rose to be subject to erosional forces. The upper portion of the Navajo Sandstone has less iron oxide and is thus whiter and weaker than the lower layers. This contributes notably to the rounder rock formations found at higher elevations and the cliffs exposed in lower canyons.

The view from the rim of Refrigerator Canyon across Zion Canyon to Cable Mountain illustrates the many canyons of the park that have been created out of the relatively flat Kolob Terrace. Running water has exploited the numerous joints that often are several miles long.

GARY LADD

JEFF GNASS

The lack of iron oxide at the upper levels of the Navajo Sandstone enhances the beauty of the Cathedral Group located just north of Zion Lodge. Throughout the river flood plain are groves of Fremont cottonwood, velvet ash, and box elder, which can only live where there is ample water.

The arch high on Bridge Mountain is located across the canyon from the Zion Canyon Visitor Center. Its fragile 156-foot-span of Navajo Sandstone is the result of weaker, less cemented rock falling out from beneath as the sandstone eroded. What remains is due to fine sand grains that have been tightly cemented together. As with all geological structures, this will eventually collapse, creating an ever-changing variety of forms. The arch may be reached by off-trail hiking and the use of basic mountaineering skills.

JOE ARNOLD JR.

LARRY ULRICH

In late afternoon The Great White Throne appears most dominant as long shadows spill into Zion Canyon and the Temple of Sinawava at our feet. This marks the northern terminus of the Zion Canyon Scenic Drive and the start of canyon widening as the Virgin River has cut through the Navajo Sandstone and begins to work on the soft shales of the Kayenta Formation

Near the Zion-Mt. Carmel Highway you will find a most unlikely place for a tree to grow! Yet for over 40 years this stunted ponderosa pine has been able to extract sufficient moisture from the spaces between the sand grains. Erosional features known as "hoodoos' result when the Navajo Sandstone weathers at different rates. Softer rock washes away easily compared to the harder rook, leaving many fanciful shapes. The slickrock section of Zion is a great place to get out and explore, letting your imagination and interest guide your feet.

RAY ATKESON

DAVID MUENCH

Spring is an excellent time of year to visit Zion and experience the waterfall at Weeping Rock. As winter snows melt on the plateau, more water develops than can soak into the Navajo Sandstone, so it flows down only to plunge out over the alcove below.

LARRY ULRICH

The West Temple at 7,810 feet is the highest peak in the southern portion of the park. From its base near Coalpits Wash it rises over 4,100 feet in a series of layers that have helped geologists study and better understand this region and the many changes that have taken place in eons past.

Early History at Zion

The Upper Virgin River drainage had been home to Anasazi Indians and Paiutes after them. In 1858, Mormon scout Nephi Johnson explored the drainage, entering Zion Canyon. His major goal was to determine if there were sufficient agricultural lands to support new farming communities along the watercourses. Based upon his favorable report, several towns were started, with some continuing to the present. Springdale was established in 1862, and took on the task of hosting the increasing number of visitors to the area after the establishment of Mukuntuweap National Monument in 1909.

NPS PHOTO

"Windows" were cut in the rock walls of Pine Creek Canyon for access and ventilation during construction of the Zion-Mt. Carmel Tunnel and Highway started in 1927.

Preliminary scaffolding crossed Pine Creek to provide access to the east portal of the Zion-Mt. Carmel Tunnel. An Erie Air Shovel was used to enlarge the pilot tunnels that were blasted into the sandstone. The resulting rock debris was hauled by narrow-gauge railcars and dumped through the galleries into the canyon below.

The dedication of the tunnel on July 4, 1930, marked the completion of the longest tunnel in the United States at that time and what many considered to be an engineering marvel.

Construction of the West Rim Trail took place in the mid-twenties as did that of some other trails in the park. This was a popular route for guided horseback trips to the West Rim, which is some 3,000 feet higher than Zion Canyon and rewarded riders with cooler temperature and unbelievable vistas. The heavy horse use and frequent afternoon thunderstorms took their toll on the trail. Soil cement was used in 1934 to preserve the tread and slow down erosion. The Civilian Conservation Corps (CCC) worked on many projects such as this during its time in Zion.

NPS PHOTO

NPS PHOTO

The Utah Parks Company, a subsidiary of the Union Pacific Railroad, built the Zion Inn and cafeteria in 1934 to provide visitors with economical accommodations in contrast to the more luxurious Zion Lodge.

*T*he Cable Mountain Draw Works used gravity to transport quality lumber from ponderosa pines growing on the plateau to the floor of Zion Canyon.

*T*he Grotto campground (now a picnic area) was the first in Zion and provided these early do-it-yourselfers with a home away from home in 1935.

*O*verleaf: The Great White Throne stands majestically behind a reflection of autumn color. Photo by David Muench.

Flora and Fauna

National parks serve as outdoor museums in which a great biological diversity of plants and animals is protected. Elevational differences of over 5,000 feet within Zion contribute to a wide variety of habitats from desert to alpine. Numerous canyons along the dissected plateau terrain provide many small niches for species to live that could not survive elsewhere in the world. The tiny Zion snail, for example, is found only in hanging gardens near the Virgin River within the park.

ERWIN & PEGGY BAUER

The American kestrel is a permanent park resident which helps to keep the rodent population in check. These birds may be seen along the Virgin River.

Boxelder trees are common within the park along streams and springlines (where water seeps from between rock layers). Although members of the maple family, their leaves turn yellow instead of red.

JEFF GNASS

"the tiny Zion snail is found only in hanging gardens near *the* **Virgin River** *within* the Park."

*M*ule deer are easy to see throughout Zion Canyon most of the year. Look in the river woodlands early and late in the day. Weaker members of the herd are a food source for mountain lions.

BECKY & GARY VESTAL

LYNN CHAMBERLAIN

*Y*ou are not likely to see a beaver along the Virgin River, but it leaves its mark on cut cottonwood trees near the Temple of Sinawava and the Court of the Patriarchs.

The Steller's jay is the only jay of the intermountain region with a crest. It prefers the conifer forests of Zion's high plateaus, but in winter can be found along the Virgin River and its tributaries.

ERWIN & PEGGY BAUER

TOM & PAT LEESON

During the summer months you may find the uncommon western bluebird in the high country of Zion where it frequents the ponderosa pine forests. In winter look for it at lower elevations along streams and in brushy areas.

C. ALLAN MORGAN

The name of the American dipper derives from its habit of flexing its legs while standing on a rock. This common year-round resident dives into streams in search of larvae that it feeds on. Nests are built near flowing water and sometimes behind a waterfall, providing protection from predators.

GARY LADD

ERWIN & PEGGY BAUER

Spotted owls are uncommon to wooded canyons within the park, but some live here all year. Do not disturb these birds, as research has been underway for several years to determine their numbers and habits.

The desert cottontail ranges throughout the lower sagebrush and juniper plant communities of the park. Although it can be seen at any time of day, it is most active from dusk until dawn.

DAVID WEINSTEIN

Even Wild Turkeys want to come out and strut their feathers. After a long absence Wild Turkeys now thrive in the Park and are often admired along the Zion Canyon Scenic Drive. Males prance with fanned tail feathers to impress hens of his harem.

In spring, hikers on the Watchman Trail are treated to early Indian paintbrush blooming in a natural rock garden. This showy member of the snapdragon family is common throughout Zion Canyon, with similar species growing in slickrock crevices and on the plateaus.

VICTOR JACKSON

GLENN VAN NIMWEGEN

Golden columbine blooms profusely in many wet areas throughout the park during the spring months. It is commonly found in May at Weeping Rock and along the Gateway to the Narrows Trail.

ERWIN & PEGGY BAUER

The coyote ranges throughout the park, but is more often heard than seen. It helps to keep rodent numbers down and works as a useful scavenger.

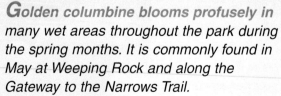

STEPHEN KRASEMANN—DRK PHOTO

Cougars or mountain lions are rarely seen in the park. They are primarily nocturnal and are usually very secretive. Mule deer, which occur in most parts of Zion, are the prime prey of this animal. Natural predation is protected by the National Park Service and results in healthier deer and cougar populations.

TOM & PAT LEESON

The bobcat ranges throughout the park, but is rarely seen due to its nocturnal and solitary habits. Dens are generally located in rocky areas near cliffs. This predator of small mammals and birds gets its name from the short, bobbed tail.

LYNN CHAMBERLAIN

DAVID MUENCH

One of the best places to see the collared lizard is along the Watchman Trail. When running, they resemble miniature dinosaurs.

Many think of Zion as a desert environment, yet in springs along the Virgin River there are small swampy areas that support watercress. Equally surprising is to see the soaring sandstone cliffs mirrored in the cool water at your feet.

When running, the collared lizard RESEMBLES a miniature dinosaur.

A showy blossom of summer is the sacred datura. The flowers open at night and usually wilt soon after sunrise. It is pollinated only by night-flying hawk and sphinx moths that are attracted to its smell and nectar.

Look for the yellow blooms of the widely distributed prickly-pear cactus during May in Zion Canyon and June at higher elevations. This hardy plant has a very efficient root system that permits it to quickly absorb rainwater following a storm. The bright red fruit, protected by tiny spines, is edible and can be used in making candy and jelly.

Kolob Canyons

The Kolob Canyons section of the park has been called "one of Utah's best kept secrets" as its beauty and diversity are not evident from Interstate 15 that passes close by. Leave I-15 at Exit 40 between Cedar City and St. George for scenic vistas that are really "a sight for sore eyes!" This northwestern part of Zion has become better known since the Kolob Canyons Visitor Center was built and donated to the park and its visitors by the Zion Natural History Association.

JOE ARNOLD JR.

The ruggedness of the Finger Canyons of the Kolob is evident from this aerial view. These Navajo Sandstone "Fingers" create the spectacular canyons that we see from below.

Isolated mesa tops provide researchers with an invaluable laboratory for the study of evolutionary processes. Like islands in the sea, these inaccessible highlands harbor unique assemblages of plant and animal species. Like other national parks, Zion has been set aside not only for enjoyment and recreation but also for the pursuit of scientific research.

TOM DANIELSEN

Kolob Arch is the reward for hiking seven miles from Lee Pass along the La Verkin Creek Trail. Electronic measurements in 1983 found this Navajo Sandstone arch to have a span of 310 feet—one of the world's two largest known freestanding arches. Most do this as an overnight hike and include such other points of interest as Beartrap Falls, Chasm Lake and/or Hop Valley.

Winter in Zion

FRED HIRSCHMANN

Winter is a spectacular time to be in Zion!
Sporadic snowstorms highlight the colored
cliffs and decorate the bare cottonwoods
along the Virgin River. A squirrel of the
conifer forests on the plateaus goes
about its daily routine to survive.
Average highs in the canyon are
near 60 degrees during the day
and about freezing at night.

LARRY BURTON

FRED HIRSCHMANN

Winter snows add yet another color to the varied rock formations. A snow fall brings on an advent of white that creates a unique opportunity for photographers to add even more drama to these already formidable scenes.

VICTOR JACKSON

Those who visit Zion during the off-season are rewarded with a wide choice of options. Cross-country skiing is possible at the higher elevations of the park after adequate snowfall. Spring is an excellent time to enjoy the trails and waterfalls from melting snow. One of the largest such falls is at the Temple of Sinawava.

Enjoying Zion

Zion has been and remains many things to a wide variety of people. Traces of Anasazi Indian cultures can be found in petroglyphs and storage granaries. In 1776, Spanish padres Dominguez and Escalante traversed the area west of Zion on their way to Monterey, California, only to be turned back by cold weather and lack of supplies. Fur trappers and traders also passed through the region in search of beaver pelts, but permanent settlements did not occur locally until Mormon pioneers arrived about 1860. The establishment of Mukuntuweap National Monument in 1909, and its subsequent renaming when Congress set aside Zion National Park in 1919, opened this incredible area to the world. The towering cliffs that seemed insurmountable obstacles to early travelers now became sanctuaries where millions can find a place of peace and relaxation.

DAVID WEINSTEIN

The Zion Canyon shuttle bus system, which began in 2000, has greatly enhanced the park experience. Prior to 2000, the traffic congestion in Zion Canyon seriously reduced visitor enjoyment of the park. Now, visitors can easily access trailheads and points of interest in Upper Zion Canyon, the most popular section of the park. The quiet, propane powered shuttle system has become a model for mass transportation efforts in other national and state parks.

When a new visitor center opened in 2000, the old visitor center became the Human History Museum. Exhibits on the park's human story and a stunning orientation program in the auditorium make this a popular stop for visitors. Viewing decks offer wonderful vistas and photo opportunities.

DAVID WEINSTEIN

PHOTOS BY DAVID WEINSTEIN

With the shuttle system came new bicycling opportunities. The Pa'rus Trail, with its wide paved surface, is the only trail in the park that allows bicycling. When the shuttle system is operating, from April – October, the reduced traffic on the Scenic Drive makes it a great place for bicycling. Cyclists should be aware that buses will not pass bicyclists, so it is important and courteous to pull to the right side and stop to let the buses pass.

Some of Zion's hikes are very strenuous and challenging. The rugged and steep route between Scout Lookout and Angels Landing should not be attempted by anyone afraid of heights and parents should find another trail for their children.

Easily accessed from the Zion Lodge, the trail to Lower Emerald Pools, is one of the most popular in the park. In wet seasons, hikers may get wet as they pass behind a waterfall.

Walk-in campsites in South Campground, near the Pa'rus Trail and Virgin River, are highly sought after by tent campers. The campsites offer out-standing views of The Watchman, one of the park's most photo-graphed peaks.

Water is fun . . .

But it can also be dangerous. Visitors enjoying the Virgin River's cool waters should be aware that they may encounter swift currents, slippery rocks, and deep water. Rainfall can turn the river into a raging, debris filled torrent within minutes. Anyone planning to venture into the river or any narrow canyon in the park should first check weather forecasts and flashflood potential ratings at one of the park's visitor centers.

DAVID WEINSTEIN

DAVID WEINSTEIN

*V*isitors can still experience Zion on horseback as the park's early visitors did. A park concessioner, located near the Zion Lodge, provides both horses and mules for guided trips within Zion Canyon. These trips are an activity the entire family can enjoy.

SUGGESTED DVD

Zion National Park Towers of Stone, 53 minutes, Whittier, California: Finley-Holiday Films.

SUGGESTED WEB SITES

www.zionpark.org

www.zionnational-park.com

www.zion.national-park.com

SUGGESTED READING

CRAWFORD, J.L. *Zion National Park: Towers of Stone.* Springdale, Utah: Zion Natural History Association, 1988.

Eves, Robert L. *Water, Rock & Time: The Geologic Story of Zion National Park.* Springdale, Utah: Zion Natural History Association, 2005.

Hayde, Frank R. and Rachlis, David. *Zion: The Story Behind the Scenery.* Wickenburg, Arizona: K.C. Publications, Inc., 2003.

Leach, Nicky. *Kolob Canyons: Zion National Park.* Springdale, Utah: Zion Natural History Association.

Woodbury, Angus M. *History of Southern Utah and Its National Parks.* Privately Published, 1950.

The Zion Canyon Shuttle Guide. SPRINGDALE, UTAH: ZION NATURAL HISTORY ASSOCIATION, 2001.

All About Zion National Park

Zion Natural History Association

The Zion Natural History Association dates back to 1931 when it was formed as the park's principal partner in providing educational material to the traveling public. ZNHA produces 37 publications centered on Zion and the surrounding area. Proceeds from the sales of publications and other interpretive items are donated to the National Park Service for use in education and research. This funding makes possible a variety of activities including Zion's popular Junior Ranger and educational outreach programs, and the printing of the Zion Map and Guide that is distributed free to arriving visitors. This private, nonprofit organization is an indispensable asset to the park and the 2.5 million annual visitors who benefit from high-quality printed information.

THE STELLER'S JAY
ERWIN & PEGGY BAUER

Contact Information

Listen to AM Radio 1610 for information on Zion National Park and the shuttle service.

Call the park at:
(435) 772-3256.

Write to:
Zion National Park
Springdale, UT 84767

Visit the park's web site at:
www.nps.gov/zion

For information on
Utah road conditions, call
(801) 964-6000.

For more information, contact:

- ZNHA, Zion National Park, Springdale, UT 84767
- Call us at (800) 635-3959 or (435) 772-3264,
- FAX (435) 772-3908,
- or visit our web site at www.zionpark.org

Junior Ranger Program

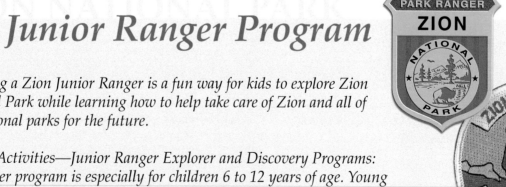

Becoming a Zion Junior Ranger is a fun way for kids to explore Zion National Park while learning how to help take care of Zion and all of our national parks for the future.

*Guided Activities—Junior Ranger Explorer and Discovery Programs:
A summer program is especially for children 6 to 12 years of age. Young explorers have a special chance to learn about Zion's natural and cultural history through games, activities, hikes, and lessons. They can earn up to three awards, including a certificate, patch, and a badge depending on which program is completed. Available Memorial Day to Labor Day weekends.*

*Self-guided Activities—Junior Ranger Activity Booklet:
Children ages 6 to 12 can earn a Junior Ranger badge by completing an activity booklet and attending a ranger-led program. Booklets are available at the Zion Canyon and Kolob Canyons Visitor Centers.*

ZION
NATIONAL PARK

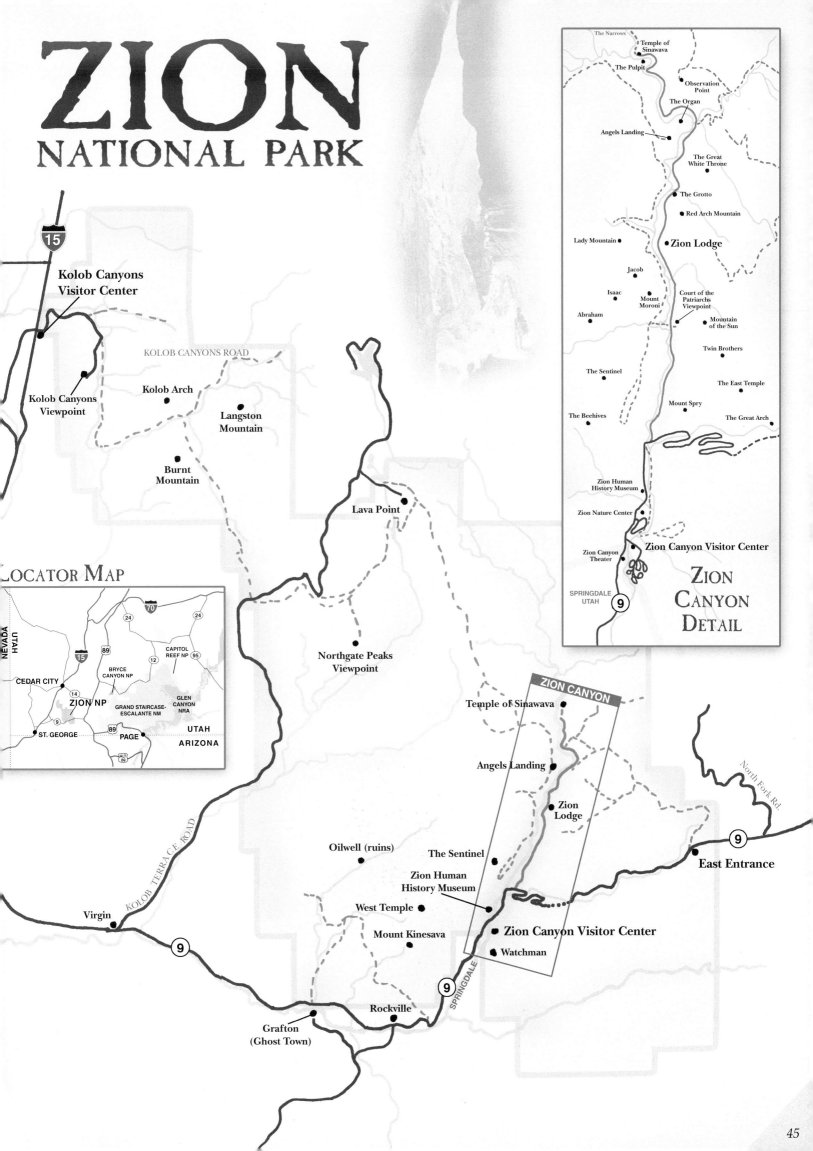

ZION CANYON DETAIL

The Narrows
Temple of Sinawava
The Pulpit
Observation Point
The Organ
Angels Landing
The Great White Throne
The Grotto
Red Arch Mountain
Lady Mountain
Zion Lodge
Jacob
Isaac
Mount Moroni
Court of the Patriarchs Viewpoint
Abraham
Mountain of the Sun
Twin Brothers
The Sentinel
The East Temple
Mount Spry
The Beehives
The Great Arch
Zion Human History Museum
Zion Nature Center
Zion Canyon Visitor Center
Zion Canyon Theater
SPRINGDALE UTAH (9)

Kolob Canyons Visitor Center

KOLOB CANYONS ROAD

Kolob Canyons Viewpoint

Kolob Arch

Langston Mountain

Burnt Mountain

Lava Point

LOCATOR MAP

NEVADA
UTAH
(70)
(24)
(89)
(24)
(12)
CAPITOL REEF NP
(95)
(15)
BRYCE CANYON NP
CEDAR CITY
(14)
ZION NP
GRAND STAIRCASE-ESCALANTE NM
GLEN CANYON NRA
(9)
(89)
ST. GEORGE
(89)
PAGE
UTAH
ALT 89
ARIZONA

Northgate Peaks Viewpoint

ZION CANYON

Temple of Sinawava

Angels Landing

Zion Lodge

North Fork Rd.

(9)

Oilwell (ruins)

The Sentinel

Zion Human History Museum

West Temple

Mount Kinesava

Zion Canyon Visitor Center

Watchman

East Entrance

KOLOB TERRACE ROAD

Virgin

(9)

SPRINGDALE

(9)

Rockville

Grafton (Ghost Town)

PETER L. KRESAN

In Zion your sense of wonder will be stimulated as you ponder the immensity of the vertical canyon walls rising from 2,000 to nearly 4,000 feet above the Virgin River. Beyond the dramatic scenery lie the forces of nature at work today and in millions of years past. Into this rugged terrain came Native Americans, explorers, Mormon pioneers, and now millions of visitors, each with special purposes. A stop at the visitor centers will bring answers from experienced personnel to help you plan your visit.

From the East Rim a golden light plays upon the rocks --- and a solitary tree. Here there is just enough moisture and nutrients to make its presence known.

Witness here a land of bold contrasts, dynamic seasons where the majesty of Nature surrounds you — Zion National Park.

FRED HIRSCHMANN

From the cold stark look of winter to the flaming sunlight of dawn – the walls beckon you to their canyon floor where virtually everything is an enjoyment of looking up in awe and pleasure.